T0068215

Even So

A Journey Through Storms

TRISHA CALDWELL

WESTBOW
PRESS®
A DIVISION OF THOMAS NELSON
& ZONDERVAN

WestBow Press books may be ordered through booksellers or by contacting:

WestBow Press
A Division of Thomas Nelson & Zondervan
1663 Liberty Drive
Bloomington, IN 47403
www.westbowpress.com
844-714-3454

Because of the dynamic nature of the Internet, any web addresses or links contained in this book may have changed since publication and may no longer be valid. The views expressed in this work are solely those of the author and do not necessarily reflect the views of the publisher, and the publisher hereby disclaims any responsibility for them.

Any people depicted in stock imagery provided by Getty Images are models, and such images are being used for illustrative purposes only. Certain stock imagery © Getty Images.

Be sure to visit TuesdaysLunchCup.com

Other Sources:
Webster's Seventh New Collegiate Dictionary
Edited by Grace Bellhy, whose own writings I hope to see in print someday!

Scriptures taken from the Holy Bible, New International Version®, NIV®. Copyright © 1973, 1978, 1984, 2011 by Biblica, Inc.™ Used by permission of Zondervan. All rights reserved worldwide. www.zondervan.com The "NIV" and "New International Version" are trademarks registered in the United States Patent and Trademark Office by Biblica, Inc.®

ISBN: 978-1-6642-5274-5 (sc)
ISBN: 978-1-6642-5273-8 (hc)
ISBN: 978-1-6642-5275-2 (e)

Library of Congress Control Number: 2022901745

Print information available on the last page.

WestBow Press rev. date: 03/23/2022

continued from back cover:

A healthy mindset doesn't change the fact that storms are hard, and it may not change the outcome. But it does change how we live the days we are given. We can choose to live in fear, or we can choose to live.

Though I didn't know her long, she was truly an inspiration: Jennifer Lilley Collins, author of <u>The In-Between is Everything</u>. While she lost her battle with cancer here on earth, she is still a winner for the legacy she left, and the lives God is still changing through her testimony. Her attitude to make the most of each day given and to glorify God gave her purpose, and she remained thankful.

Thankfulness, an important part of any journey, is "being conscious of a benefit received." It is choosing to find things for which to be thankful. It doesn't stop the storms, it's not a 'fake it 'til you make it'. But it is part of the recipe for giving our cares to God – the act of giving our worries to Him *by prayer and petition, with thanksgiving (Philippians 4:6)* reduces the anxiety, bringing it back down to size when looking through God's eyes. For no storm is too big, or too small, for Him. *Rejoice in the Lord always. I will say it again, rejoice (Philippians 4:4)* is about the deep joy in our lives that can only come from God, who fills every void and strengthens us when we trust in Him. *Read Philippians, where Paul writes about his journey of joy and thankfulness while held captive in prison.*

Thankfulness can come from a somber heart or flow from hidden tears as we hold onto Jesus and seek Him. It can come from a heart that doesn't understand but chooses to trust in the Lord anyway. *Trust in the Lord with all your heart and lean not on your own understanding. In all your ways submit to Him and He will make your paths straight (Proverbs 3:5–6).* In this verse, it doesn't promise our paths will be made easy, but straight as we walk with God and trust His ways.

It's hard to understand why some seem to go through more storms than others. But I've learned that it's not about comparing who's had it harder; it's not about fair. It's just life – it is what it is. I think about Jennifer, about her family and friends in their grief. And the tears flow. Tears are cleansing, healing, allowing us to move forward, to feel, to forgive, to love.

In <u>No More Faking Fine</u>, Esther Fleece writes:

"God wants our sad. Maybe you've never been admonished by a courtroom judge or threatened by a parent *[or faced a traumatic experience]*, but I'll bet you can remember some of the pivotal moments that taught you to fake fine to one degree or another. Maybe you grew up being told that boys don't cry, so you stuffed your pain deep inside. Maybe you had all the right clothes and all the right friends and all the right grades, but you never invited friends over – because then they'd know the mess you lived with at home. Maybe you were told that if you just did certain things and clicked your heels, you'd have the good life you've always wanted – you know, the one the prosperity gospel is always promising – but you haven't even glimpsed it on the horizon.

The story our culture tells us – and even some misguided churches – is that health, wealth, and prosperity can and should be ours. As Americans, we are often led to believe we are entitled to these things. We are led to believe life should be easy, and we should be happy. So, of course, when life crashes hard, we believe something must be wrong with us. ...

Lament is one of those words we don't use very much today. It is simply expressing honest emotions to God when life is not going as planned. The majority of us have said or heard predictable clichés in times of suffering:

"If God brings you to it, He'll bring you through it."
"It could have been worse."
"Everything happens for a reason."

This is not a biblical way of thinking, nor is it a biblical way of dealing. We say these things because, somewhere along the way, we lost the biblical language of lament. We have not discovered the beauty in sorrow, so we try to get out of pain as quickly as possible – and we expect others to do so as well. But life will let all of us down, and we need a way to talk about it. …

God is not up there minimizing our pain and comparing it to others who have it worse than we do. God wants all pain to be surrendered to Him, and He has the capacity to respond to it all with infinite compassion. What's more, lament is a pathway. Honest expression to God makes way for God to come and work His real healing."

Lament is a process. Healing is a process. And let's make it clear that healing isn't always a reference to physical healing, nor does it mean the healing will be completed here on earth. Our perfect bodies are promised in heaven. Let's also be clear that, even so, God continues to work all things together for the good of those who love Him (Romans 8:28). No where in this passage does God say all things will *be* good or easy for those who love Him. It says He takes all of it – the good, the bad, the hard, the easy – and works it together for our good and His glory. We are broken, we need fixed, and we aren't meant to do it on our own.

Thankfulness. Sadness. We can be sad and thankful at the same time. We can be frustrated and still trust God. And we can face the journey when we walk with God.

As you read, I hope you will align your own journey to these pages, not discounting the challenges or harsh realities of your storm, but holding on to Christ *Even So;* for He is with us through the storms.

Dedication

To my heavenly Father who has never let me go no matter the storm, walking with me in every journey, always faithful and true. "For Jesus Christ is the same yesterday, today and forever." Hebrews 13:8

Lord, You are my rock and my fortress, my God in whom I trust.
Psalm 18:1–2

To my husband who walks beside me, never letting a storm come between us. You trust God so easily, reminding me, "God's got this."

Shawn, you are amazing. Thank you for loving me unconditionally and walking each journey with me, never losing hope and being the calm in each day. I am undeservedly blessed, and I thank God for you!

To my Mom who was by my side pouring into me, just being here, and watching over our family so they didn't get lost in the overwhelming storm that so suddenly became our reality.

Mom, you didn't even hesitate – you were right here taking action and knowing what we needed. No matter how tired you were, you were always ready to serve. You are such a blessing and I thank God for you!

To my children who never stopped believing, and spent precious time with me, building me up and challenging me to live each day one day at a time. You continue to be a blessing to me.

"Children are a heritage from the Lord, offspring a reward from Him." Psalm 127:3

I wish I had room to list everyone: family members, friends, and friends of friends. Thank you to all who prayed for us, reached out to us ready to help at any given moment, and supported us in so many ways. The joy you bring to my life even now – I am forever grateful, and I thank God for you!

Contents

Introduction

July 3, 2016 When someone asks how we are doing, how do we respond? Are we honest with our response? And do they really want to know, or are they just making small talk as they walk past? I often respond with "Good." And I mean it because I believe that I am okay and God is good all the time, even in the midst of the storms.

But how do I actually feel at that moment? That could be a totally different answer. For instance, today I feel grumpy. I don't want to be bothered, I just want quiet time, and I don't have anything left to pour into anyone. But do I honestly want to tell someone that when they are just walking past me? Probably not, unless it's a good friend who really wants to know how I am doing.

On the other hand, it is so important that we be honest about how we are doing. Using my 'I'm grumpy' example, I have found that when I verbally admit how I feel, it takes the edge off when it's a 'down' feeling, and it allows me to share the happiness when it's an 'up' feeling. So now that I have told you I feel grumpy today, suddenly the grumpiness has lessened because I let it out of my dark stuff-it-down-inside self, and a new light shines on the day. I still don't want to be bothered much, and I don't have much to pour into anyone, but the grumpy feeling has lessened, and I am less likely to snap at someone. I've heard this referred to as "soul words", stating how you feel and what you need. It's not only freeing because we have let it out, but it also helps those around us be on the same page and know what we need. And we will find that family or friends are happy to be there for us. They just want to know what we honestly need.

God is good even in the storms has been my theme through this journey. Turning to God for strength, encouragement, guidance, and deliverance, is truly the key. On these grumpy days, I tell God I feel grumpy. I feel Him smiling at me because He already knows, and He is glad I'm talking to Him about how I feel. He can work in and through me because I let it go and asked that His Spirit be in control of me.

How about you? How are you today, and what are you feeling? Tell God. Tell a friend. You can still have a good day .... it doesn't have to be a bubbly day or a perfect day. It can just be a quiet day, or I-made-it-through day.

Blessings to you as you read this!

"You, Lord, keep my lamp burning;
my God turns my darkness into light."
Psalm 18:28

"So do not fear, for I am with you; do not be dismayed,
for I am your God. I will strengthen you and help you;
I will uphold you with My righteous right hand."
Isaiah 41:10

"But I trust in Your unfailing love;
my heart rejoices in Your salvation.
I will sing the Lord's praise,
for He has been good to me."
Psalm 13:5–6

As you read through my journal, you will notice some dates say 'website' next to them. During my journey, there was a website for people to sign up for meals, and where I could also keep people updated on how I was doing. So there will be a few similar journals.

Even So

A Journey Through Storms

I love the sky Lord, all the parts of it. You speak to me there – of beauty and magnificence that go beyond what our naked eye can see. I wonder if You have ever painted it the same way twice: the different shades of the sunrise and sunset, the different shapes in the clouds, the different streaks of lightning, and how the shades of blue cover the sky in different patterns – these all speak of Your beauty and magnificence. You are in all of this, and I love You!

Even so, You are good!

Psalm 19

April 23, 2016 I am limited on writing due to the pain in my right arm and shoulder, so journaling might be brief sometimes. But God is good and faithful in all this. His plan is perfect, and He is always with me.

December 4, 2015, I was in a parade where, for the two-mile walk, we did God Rods to the song "Arise My Love," by Newsong (this is 'movement for nonmovers': YouTube > God Rods Salt & Light Ministries Videos). In the middle of the night I woke up with awful pain in my shoulder and thought *what did I do*? I went to see my chiropractor the next day for the normal therapy we do when my old injury kicks in, but after a month we knew something else was wrong.

Long story short, we went from x-ray to cortisone to MRI to bone scan to bone biopsy, to learn there is a cancerous tumor *in* my bone. Praising God – it is not in my bone marrow or lymph nodes, and blood counts were good, so it was contained for the time being.

Then we did a PET scan – more cancer showed up in several bone areas – the left shoulder and clavicle bone area. I bawled and bawled and bawled. This is not what we expected at all, especially since I had no other symptoms. How did we get from inflaming an old injury to cancer, in the course of a couple months? And yet in all this we still knew, and felt, and held onto God's peace. God's amazing love and grace and peace, which only He can explain - He is God, and He is Sovereign. Writing about Him brings peace and hope.

Our oncologist wanted to move quickly on this aggressive cancer, and one week later I am sitting here in the hospital with inpatient chemo. Talk about turning your world upside down! And still God is good. We praise him in this storm, for His plans are perfect. There is a reason we are here. And thankfulness is a beautiful way to move through the tough times.

Psalm 16

A *miktam* of David.

¹ Keep me safe, my God,
for in you I take refuge.

² I say to the LORD, "You are my Lord;
apart from you I have no good thing."
³ I say of the holy people who are in the land,
"They are the noble ones in whom is all my delight."
⁴ Those who run after other gods will suffer more and more.
I will not pour out libations of blood to such gods
or take up their names on my lips.

⁵ LORD, you alone are my portion and my cup;
you make my lot secure.
⁶ The boundary lines have fallen for me in pleasant places;
surely I have a delightful inheritance.
⁷ I will praise the LORD, who counsels me;
even at night my heart instructs me.
⁸ I keep my eyes always on the LORD.
With him at my right hand, I will not be shaken.

⁹ Therefore my heart is glad and my tongue rejoices;
my body also will rest secure,
¹⁰ because you will not abandon me to the realm of the dead,
nor will you let your faithful one see decay.
¹¹ You make known to me the path of life;
you will fill me with joy in your presence,
with eternal pleasures at your right hand.

Have you ever wrestled with God? Did you think He was mad at you? Maybe that depends on why we are wrestling. I have had my share of wrestling matches with God, usually over wanting to know why, or wanting answers before His perfect timing.

Jacob wrestled with God, and God blessed him. Jesus wrestled in the Garden with the path He chose to take, and God strengthened Him. They were seeking God's face, His path, His truth, searching Him out. God was not angry with them, but rather grew them through it. In their weakness God proved His strength and their need for Him.

I do think there are times when God is angry with the things we do, the paths we choose that do not follow Him. But praise God we live in the age of grace! As believers in Christ, when we confess our sins He forgives us and cleanses us. Consequences may linger but that's not anger, it's discipline.

When we talk to God, may we be reverent in our questionings and in being real with Him. He already knows everything, so we aren't going to surprise Him. He wants us to talk with Him and listen to Him. Trust and obey. He will help us through.

Even so, God is gracious

Hebrews 4:14–16, 1 John 1:8–9

April 15, 2016 Today I learned that the cancer is in other bone areas, not just my right shoulder, and we will need to do inpatient chemo, and I won't be allowed to work. So many things go through my mind all at once, as my hubby sits with his hand on me. What about my family, what about our income, what about all the things I take care of and the people at work getting paid since I do payroll? I call to God in my mind as the tears pour down my face. And God is right here holding me up, reminding me we had asked that He guide us in the right decision for treatment – guide us and our oncologist, who is also a believer. The tears slow, and Shawn and I look at each other as we prayerfully make the decision to do chemo. And then I cry the whole ride home.

April 16, 2016 I'm doing better, feeling God's presence and hearing Him assure me that He has a beautiful plan. Standing in my kitchen, I say to God, "We know we are not in control; You are. Obviously, we really are *not* in control! And don't let me stand in Your way Lord. I want what *You* want." Now to start telling people - - shocking people really. We haven't said much up to this point, as we weren't expecting this at all! Our kids are doing okay – our youngest got out a really good cry the night before. And she stays by my side each night to make sure I'm okay.

Our second son needs more time to process – it is hard for him to be okay with this, as he thinks he should be feeling more emotion right away, with this being such big news. We talked about it being okay to process differently, and I assured him that he is showing feelings – every time he asks how I am, if I need anything, or if he can help. And our oldest is probably the hardest to tell because he is at college. He knows I have shoulder trouble and a tumor, but not about the other cancer spots. We talked for a while, and he asked questions. He also has friends at college who have had loved ones go through cancer, and he can talk to them. We will stay in touch over the days, so he knows how I'm doing and that I am okay. Hopefully, when he comes home for the summer and sees me doing okay, he will feel even more encouraged.

April 17, 2016 Church was amazing today! God's presence so filled that place, and we all worshipped from our hearts with such a belief that He is our Sustainer, our Healer, our Overcomer. God continues to fill us with His peace that we are in His will, and He has a perfect plan in all this. We also had a great family day!

April 18, 2016 This is the day I had to let my boss and co-workers know. God keeps opening door after door for me to share the news with hope, with a positive attitude, with a *God's got this* belief that has a lot of people scratching their heads. It makes me smile even as I write this because I count it a privilege to be able to share that God is alive and well, He is still working, He is using this for good, and He is in control. Also today I met the other oncologist who is part of the second team working with me. As he was expounding on some of the details – which is very helpful, because this is a LOT of information we are taking in so quickly – he checked my right shoulder and asked, "Did anyone tell you to not lift anything with that arm?" I related that I was told to use it very little and be extra careful because the bone is probably very weak. But no one said to not lift at all. He said, "You can lift a pen. That's all." I actually laughed because it caught me off guard, but then realized the seriousness of what he said, so I started writing left-handed as much as possible. I am already the one-armed bandit (as I call myself) for most things now. But this adds another layer of challenges because I don't want to break my shoulder.

Thankfully, my hubby and kids are great helpers and continually step up to the plate to make sure I am taken care of. Our daughter keeps asking, "Should you be doing that?" To which my response is, "If I can lefty it, I'm gonna do it." Then we laugh.

We laugh about a lot of things; it's so refreshing and healing and wonderful to laugh, even in tough times. Probably *more* so in the tough times. I truly believe this laughter is a gift from God and He has filled our home with it to keep a positive, believing environment. We laugh about my lefty attempts (which are getting better), and that my hair will fall out (we're going to see who has the better looking bald head – me or my hubby), and we laugh when I take the pain pill that makes me sleepy and out of it – we call it my loopy pill. We laugh playing games, we joke around with each other, and we keep on living. Life is hard, but we keep on living. It's what God wants, and it is Him living through us. Laugh today!

April 19 to April 21, 2016 These next days are a blur of making sure things are organized and taken care of for my family, enjoying my mom being here from NC, organizing things at work for those covering my job the next several months, and enjoying family time and making certain our kids are talking, and will talk, about the cancer.

April 22, 2016 Nervous, yet at peace, Shawn and my mom and I head to the hospital for the pre-treatment, a protein treatment they have been using before chemo to help reduce inflammation and joint damage. While it is not necesssarily common to have a strong allergic reaction to this, I did (go figure)! I was okay at first, as they start in small doses and gradually increase, while continually monitoring you. At the third increase (two hours into the treatment) I noticed my chest feeling funny. I took a drink and realized my throat was closing, and I got dizzy and nauseous. So my mom got the nurse, and they immediately stopped the treatment and gave an allergy medicine and the EpiPen, while I took deep breaths, asking God to help me not pass out or throw up. No more of that treatment for the day! (It is understandable to have a reaction, as the body considers the protein injection a foreign substance the first time. Once they are able to get a full dose in – which will be inpatient the next time so they can do it *very* slowly, the body accepts it).

We had to wait a while for a room, so my mom and I enjoyed just hanging together. And several hours later I got my private room, with a nice view of downtown Pittsburgh. All the little things are such a blessing! Shawn left for a while to take care of the kids, and he brought them back to visit. Now my wonderful, loving husband is staying the night with me. Just having him here is such a comfort as we have no idea what each moment will bring. I am so blessed by this wonderful man God has given me!

April 23, 2016 My mom came back to hang with me today, and Shawn and our daughter got to enjoy a Pittsburgh Penguins hockey playoff game! What an awesome gift! Just two days ago, one of Shawn's acquaintances approached him with a couple tickets to the game. Shawn was so excited, and yet hesitant, since I am just starting treatments. But we decided he should absolutely go! Just because life changes or turns upside down, doesn't mean it should stop. And what beautiful timing, as he got to take our daughter and they had such a great father-daughter day! *Exactly what the doctor ordered* – God knew. Then I got to see them after the game before they went home.

While they were at the game, my mom and I were learning more about relaxing in God's timing - - it takes a while, a few hours, to make the chemotherapy recipe specific to one's treatment. The mix has to be perfect, including taking into consideration the patient's size, weight, body mass. And then the mix has to be double, *and* triple checked before they can use it. So at first it's like, *What's taking so long with getting the chemo going.* But the nurses and doctors are so good here about keeping us informed and answering our questions, they are explaining things to us before we ask! Then my wonderful mom spends the night with me.

> "Our mouths were filled with laughter,
> our tongues with songs of joy.
> Then it was said among the nations,
> 'The Lord has done great things for them.'"
> Psalm 126:2

How quickly do we turn our back on God's path when we do not understand? We think that as soon as we say, "Yes God, I will do what You ask of me," our understanding of why He asked should be immediate. We turn around looking for what *we* understand because that is what makes sense. But God says to lean on His understanding and trust His way. And we put our hands to our ears and say, "La-la-la-la, I can't hear You." Then we wonder why our way didn't work.

"But God, I listened to You, and this is what I understood," we cry. Or should we cry out with, "God, I do not understand in my own mind, but I hold onto Your understanding and Your wisdom in this."

When we hold onto man's wisdom we distrust God's wisdom, keeping the Spirit from opening our eyes and heart and guiding our faith to be certain of what we do *not* see. (Hebrews 11:1)

And how do we respond when God does give us a deeper, fuller view of the picture He is painting? Do we thank Him? Do we praise Him and give GOD the glory? Or do we make it sound like we are something special because we grasp the vision, like we have this great gift of understanding? May we not forget that it is God who gives us our understanding – it is His Spirit working in and through us. ALL the glory must go back to Him!

Even so, God is wisdom

Proverbs 3

April 25, 2016 Things that make me cry:

- Surprising news of cancer and needing more intense chemo
- Not being with my family every day, and what they are going through in processing everything
- How amazing my husband and kids - how resilient, and their faith and trust in God. Their testimony to others
- God's peace, faithfulness and continual promise that He is working with me and He's got this. It continues to surpass all understanding
- All the amazing friends and prayer warriors who truly, genuinely are here for us and help us
- My mom's exceptional love and care for our kids – thinking of beautiful ways to help them through, teach them how to help me, make them feel comforted and loved, and keep structure and routine in their lives
- Family and friends respecting my privacy, and always being ready to help
- The extreme pain in my arm and shoulder
- God's beautiful words: words of promise, peace, hope, strength, comfort and love, no matter what each day brings
- God's constant provision, and His tenderness and love

April 25, 2016 (website post) Hello Everyone! It's great to catch up with you and let you know we are doing good, my family and I! The treatments have been going well with no side effects, and other than the pain in my shoulder where the cancer is the worst, I am fine. I had x-rays today so they can hopefully see what kind of damage the tumor might be causing in my shoulder bone and start formulating a plan for repairing it as we move forward.

The cancer center team here has been truly wonderful! They have created a genuine, positive, caring environment and continually take great care of me. What a blessing! We are so grateful for God's provision.

Your words of encouragement, your prayers and thoughts, mean so very much to all of us. God bless you as you reach out, and may you feel our sincere appreciation. Sometimes the nervousness kicks in, and every time God sends blessings and encouragement from His Word and from you. He is amazing!

We love you all. God bless you!

"Lord, let Your ear be attentive to the prayer of this
Your servant and to the prayer of Your servants
who delight in revering Your name."
Nehemiah 1:11

April 26, 2016 Dear Lord, You have given me a beautiful view of the city as I sit with You this morning. Just another picture of Your beauty. And yet, not 'just' … for your beauty goes beyond words when we let ourselves really stop and see. Even in the storms Lord, You bring beauty!

As I sit here listening to the sounds, the voices, the teams of doctors and nurses in this cancer center working together to make us as comfortable as possible and help us through the healing process, I hear and see the beauty of God's provision in their laughter, their genuine care, and the positive environment they have created. A beautiful reminder that You care Lord, and we are not forgotten.

When nervousness kicks in and I want my anxious heart to rest in You and calm down, You speak life into my very soul, reminding me You are here, and You can handle this.

When a friend sends a verse at just the right time, or says, "I'm praying for you; stay strong," or when the tears need to fall from the emotions, or laughter erupts 'cause my husband is entertaining me - - in all of this is beauty. To feel is beautiful!

And how about when someone is in for treatments and they can't get out of bed, not even to use the bathroom. How is there beauty? It's in the gentle care of the nurse who goes to help them. It's in the time the aide or doctor gives them by pulling up a chair and talking with them.

The beauty is here in the storms. Just like the rain and thunderstorms outside. Some days they seem to go on and on and we just want sunshine. But don't miss the beauty: time to relax with a good book, playing extra games with the family, playing in the rain, seeing the rainbow, listening for which clap of thunder is louder. And when the storms are devastating – where is the beauty? This is not a perfect world, and there is a lot of sadness and devastation that can easily overtake. But God wants to help us through this too. It is where we really grow and where He can strengthen our trust and faith the best. So I have found the beauty in feeling His arms around me, knowing I'm not alone. And beauty in the community of people who come together to help, and in those God provides who have been through this before. There is beauty in reaching out to others going through difficulty – it takes our eyes off ourselves all the time, so we can breathe and heal.

The beauty is here when we want to see it.

"One thing I ask of the Lord,
this only do I seek:
that I may dwell in the house of the Lord
all the days of my life,
to gaze on the beauty of the Lord
and to seek Him in His temple."
Psalm 27:4

We must die daily to ourselves and what we want, so Christ can fill us with what is best. Daily. "Really, Lord? Every day, even when I'm just so sure my way is working and right?"

Yet it's when we let go and let God, that things become clearer. It might become clear little by little, or clear right away. Though it will never be fully clear, we must trust His timing and plan, for He is faithful! As long as we are fighting for control our judgment is clouded, our eyes blinded, and our hearts weary.

God will not force His will on us, though He will keep bringing us back around to His plan if we keep swerving, for His plan is right. "Whoever wants to save their life will lose it, but whoever loses their life for Me will save it." Luke 9:24

The precious blood of His Son, His sacrifice and saving grace through it all, is His gift to us every day! Oh Lord, thank You for Your gift, for Your love, and for my free will. I give it back to You, laying down my desires and taking up Your will as You help me trust Your ways.

Even so, You deserve my trust

Matthew 16:24–26, Luke 9:23–25

April 27, 2016 I am so excited today! I get to go home with my family! It's been six days away from them, but for the visits. Oh to be home!

As I walked the halls this morning to get exercise, I kept praying for all the patients. Some are young, some are older. Many seem to be bedridden, though I'm just guessing because I don't see them up or walking. And I wonder their story, their suffering, how bad their diagnosis might be, how promising their treatment, etc. It is good to see family and friends here to visit them. It is not easy to be here in bed, strapped to medicine bags for so many days! And some have been here longer than me, I think.

Maybe this is my purpose today, to walk the halls and pray for each of them – that they would all receive a dose of encouragement today, and that they would be open to it and able to receive. For God loves them.

"Therefore, encourage one another
and build each other up,
just as in fact you are doing."
1 Thessalonians 5:11

April 28, 2016 (website post) So I've been home for a day now and am just loving being with my family! It was enjoyable playing a game, watching a movie, and just laughing together after being gone six days.

I am still doing well, grateful to not be sick, and except for the water retention from the medicine, and the pain in my shoulder, I'm feeling good. While I was in for the treatments, my bone specialist was able to determine that I do have a fracture in my shoulder from the tumor. But praise God it is a clean fracture, and Lord willing it will heal on its own. I just have to wear a sling for a while and be patient and very careful.

Patient … that may be a challenge. I enjoy being active, not one to just sit around, so this may get interesting over these next months. But you have already sent some care packages with things to occupy my mind and time while I need to rest. And reading the Bible and praying for all of you is a beautiful way to spend time, too.

I hope this finds you having a blessed day and finding the good in your day no matter what is happening in your life. Remember, there is beauty and there is good – don't be afraid to look for it!

Keep Shining!

May 2, 2016 (website post) Hello! And Happy Monday! It's going to be a beautiful week just because we want it to be! As I think about things today and wrap my mind around everything happening, it would be good to share things I've experienced so far. As we stay positive in the Lord, in whom is our hope, we also want to be real about what is happening.

Things I've experienced so far:

- Nervousness at each new thing.
- Many tears the first day we got the news that cancer was in more bone areas than just my shoulder.
- Peace – God's amazing peace that He is working in the midst of this, and He's got this.
- A LOT of pain in my shoulder the last several months.
- Trouble sleeping because of the pain. I'm going on 4 months of sleeping in a recliner, and only being able to sleep a couple hours at a time before the pain wakes me. (Sleeping is getting easier as the tumor is starting to shrink – Yay!)
- Allergic reaction to the protein-based pre-medication they give before being admitted for chemo. My chest and throat felt like they were closing, and we did Benadryl and EpiPen right away in order to clear it. It worked quickly, but what I remember is sitting there willing myself to not pass out and to not throw up, and continually saying, "God, I know You've got this. I trust You."
- A desire to help everyone else not worry.
- Relief when my hubby stayed with me the first night in the hospital, then my mom the second night, and my hubby the third

night. We had a wonderful time just hanging together and talking and laughing, and just their presence gave me comfort those first couple nights. I am so grateful for them and their sacrifice to sleep on a small pull-out couch.

- Off-the-charts-more-than-ever pain when they had to do another x-ray of my shoulder after a couple days of chemo.
- Gratefulness when the bone specialist relayed that, though the tumor did cause a fracture in my shoulder, it is clean and should heal on its own.
- Wonderful sense of love and support as so, so many family and friends are praying and lifting us all up in prayer. Simple as it might seem, the amount of comfort, encouragement, and strength just in everyone praying for us is truly beyond words to describe right now.
- Constipation.
- Nausea. But no getting sick, and the nausea was easily controlled.
- Rash on my face – just a side effect, but it is ugly and itchy, and ugly. Did I mention it's ugly? It's hard to look at myself in the mirror, but I keep remembering that this will pass. Thankfully my hubby didn't marry me just for my looks!
- No shower; only washing up. Oh to have a refreshing shower!
- Days of being really tired and taking naps all day long.
- A great team of doctors and nurses working on my behalf: good with communicating, and organized with everything I need, including different ways to help my family in dealing with this.
- A healing environment in the hospital; they have created a very genuine, very caring, very positive atmosphere.
- Water retention – twenty pounds! UGH! Which gives me a new understanding of what someone goes through who deals with water retention on a daily basis. This is definitely at the top of the "don't want to experience that again" list!

- Laughter – at my waddling around with this water retention … I swear I look like a penguin waddling around and feel like the Sta-Puff Marshmallow! Also laughter at the thought of losing my hair … my mom wants to get me a red wig, and I want to know who has the prettier bald head – me or my hubby. Laughter when I get loopy after taking a stronger pain pill when needed. Laughter while playing games, joking around, and just enjoying life.

Life keeps going no matter what we are going through. I believe laughter is a gift from God, helping us heal, relax, and see things with a less dramatic perspective; we know He's got this! No matter what you are experiencing, let yourself feel. Give the feelings to God so He can help you keep living. And laugh today! Love you all

May 3, 2016 (website post) So this is the third somewhat sleepless night I have had (how do people who suffer with insomnia do this?), partly due to the prednisone I'm on for the allergic reaction to dairy that I didn't realize I was ingesting, and partly because I can't get comfortable – tired of the recliner but can't lie flat for the shoulder pain. After letting the tears flow from frustration and just wanting to sleep – actually, *while* the tears flowed – I cried out to God to help me; "You are my Rock Lord, no matter what, no matter how hard this gets, no matter the storm."

He quieted my heart, relaxed my mind, and helped my body calm down and be okay with the recliner again. As I sit here playing solitaire on my phone, I continue to thank God for at least being able to relax and rest. I pray for family and friends, lifting them up with all my heart. And I am reminded it is better to be thankful and appreciate the rest, than to worry that I'm not sleeping a certain number of hours. The worry would just exert unnecessary energy anyhow.

When it comes down to it, Jesus is my ultimate healer. So even if all the 'right' things that one is supposed to do in order to heal are not the things that are happening, Jesus can do anything. He can work in and through anything. And as I trust Him and be thankful, He will do amazingly more than I could ask or imagine. I will not be afraid. God's got this, and we choose to be thankful in everything, for this is God's will for us.

The cool thing is, God's Word – the Bible – still applies today. He is real! May you be blessed today.

Love Trish

Psalm 18:2 "The Lord is my rock, my fortress, my deliverer; my God is my rock in whom I take refuge, my shield and the horn of my salvation, my stronghold."

Ephesians 3:20–21a "Now to Him who is able to do immeasurably more than we could ask or imagine, according to *His* power that is at work in us, *to Him* be glory."

1 Thessalonians 5:16–18 "Rejoice always, pray continually, give thanks in all circumstances; for this is God's will for you in Christ Jesus."

"The Lord confides in those who fear Him; He makes His covenant known to them." Psalm 25:14

I love the intimacy with God that is promised here: as we trust Him, revere Him as Sovereign God, He confides in us. Oh to hear His promises directly spoken to our heart, our very soul, words cannot express! Just as He promises in Jeremiah 29:13, "You will seek Me, and find Me when you seek Me with all your heart."

And yet that bubble of deep joy can be popped so quickly by pride. How often I have found myself like Joseph in Genesis, quick to say, "I know what God is going to do." Someone tape my mouth shut! God shared visions and dreams with Joseph of things to come, ways God was going to use him. And when I read his story, I often wonder if he was somewhat prideful when he told his family they would bow down to him.

Not saying he meant it to sound like that, I'm just wondering. Unfortunately, pride has a way of sneaking into the room before we realize we opened the door. But I love how God brought it all together for good, between lessons learned and putting Joseph in the right place at the right time to help save God's people, and others.

Let us so completely enjoy the blessing of being close to God, allowed such intimacy in knowing Him – though we will never fully understand Him. Let us not ruin it by pride.

Close our mouths, Lord. Humble our hearts. And may we only move ahead with what You tell us to do and say each day.

Even so, You hold us all

Genesis 37–45; John 15:9–11; Romans 8:28

May 7, 2016 (website post) First of all, HAPPY MOTHER'S DAY to all the moms, and women who have been like a mom to someone! May you continue to be an inspiration to those around you and have a super blessed day!

So I obviously have a lot of time to just be still … and reflect … and thank God for each of you … and more. Not that my brain ever stops. Sometimes I wish I had an off switch! But I have been thinking about all the people God has placed in my path who have dealt or are dealing with cancer, and how many of them have said, "What's going on with this cancer stuff?"

History does tend to repeat itself, does it not? I think back to the histories of epidemic diseases, and the stories of all the research to find cures, and I think this is no different. I also believe the epidemic is related to the chemicals and toxins allowed in our food, drink, skin care, cosmetics, etc. It's no secret anymore, the junk being put into our bodies. Which of course raises the question, "What about the chemicals going into the body for chemo treatments?"

My husband and I had the same questions; we prayed about what the best route would be for treating my bone cancer. Yet in the midst of these questions and research, one thing remains absolutely certain – God has been clear in leading us to take the chemo route.

"That doesn't make sense," you might say. "Why would God lead you to go a route that puts such stuff in your body when there are other options?" And this is where it simply comes down to: God is Sovereign, He is in control, and He can work in and through ANYTHING! If He wants to heal me through chemo treatments, He will. If He wants to heal through natural treatments, or not until heaven, He will. He asks us to live by faith, take each step *in* faith, completely trust and obey Him, and His plan will prevail.

Maybe I'm supposed to do the chemo because He wants me to be here for someone else who in the hospital at the same time, be an encouragement to someone who is experiencing the same kind of treatment or side effects, or so very many other reasons that could be! But one thing remains true – He knows what He is doing and we must choose to trust Him. So we take this step in faith believing that His plan is perfect.

I've watched people live an extremely healthy lifestyle and die of a massive heart attack, or live a rather unhealthy lifestyle and live to be an energetic eighty-eight years old. We strive to do everything we can to live healthy and take care of ourselves and make right choices - - and we *are* supposed to do this. God expects our best and our obedience. Yet it doesn't mean we won't have issues; His ways are higher than ours and He works how He chooses.

So if God has called you to be an expert in health and nutrition and set the example for others, if God has called you to be a doctor or pharmacist, if God has called you to be a writer or secretary or accountant - - whatever it might be, can I encourage you to do your best FOR HIM? He knows what He is doing, and He wants to use you and bring about a beautiful plan for your life. Even when it doesn't make sense, He is in control. I pray you let Him lead you today.

"For the word of the Lord is right and true;
He is faithful in all He does."
Psalm 33:4

May 9, 2016 I trust You Lord to work through this. I don't want to stand in Your way. I want to be a vessel through which You can work. This is all about You Lord. Thank You for using me. May Your words flow through me today. I love You Lord.

May 12, 2016 (website post) I've been wanting to add a journal the last couple days, but each time I tried, the words just weren't there. What else can I share during these days when I am more tired, needing extra rest, and truly have no desire to do anything? But God knows what He wants shared ... He just needed to humble me more.

Galatians 6:2 "Carry each other's burdens, and in this way you will fulfill the law of Christ" – to love our neighbors as ourselves. Why can this be easier to DO than RECEIVE? As a wife and mom, I want to be there for my family and take care of them. However, in turn I need to let them be here for me. It's hard for me to be okay with needing help. I want to be strong enough, but then I don't let God be my strength, and what I do isn't as meaningful as what God can do.

A couple friends shared with me just this morning about this same lesson being learned through their health journey. The one word that sums it all up is '*humbling*'. It is good to be humbled. This is when God does His best work in us.

And God *wants* to pour into us! He knows our desires and needs, and that we need to be continually poured into so we can then pour into others, carrying their burdens. I am also reminded that it helps my family cope, when they know they are doing something to help me. Just like Moses in Deuteronomy 1:12, "How can I bear your problems and your burdens and your disputes all by myself?" Asking for help is a good thing.

So today I encourage you, along with myself, to be willing to receive *from* others, as much as giving to them. Thank you all for standing with us and carrying our burdens together. We pray God is pouring into you and you are receiving it!

"Praise be to the Lord, to God our Savior, who daily bears our burdens." Psalm 68:19

May 13, 2016 I've really struggled this week with going back in for the next round. I've felt 'off' all week, and very tired, and I realize now that part of it is, I don't want to go back into the hospital. I have some nervousness and apprehension about how I might respond this time. Will I be sick? Will my hair completely fall out? It's already started; it really came out today in handfuls! At least I have a lot of hair and already wear it short. It just looks like I thinned it down. But I think the biggest thing is, this time more is expected of our kids, and of Shawn. Not that they can't do this; and it is good for them. It comes down to my letting go even more. Just when I think I have relinquished control and put them in God's hands, He shows that I am doing better but still have more letting go to do.

I'm reminded of what Paul said in Philippians 3:12–14 "Not that I have already obtained all this, or have already arrived at my goal, but I press on to take hold of that for which Christ Jesus took hold of me. Brothers and sisters, I do not consider myself yet to have taken hold of it. But one thing I do: Forgetting what is behind and straining toward what is ahead, I press on toward the goal to win the prize for which God has called me heavenward in Christ Jesus."

Lord, You are with me and I love You! *You* are in control and I need You - - I really, really, really need You!

The simplicity of sharing with one another and being together, relating and fellowshipping. We were made for relationships. Think about Christ – He wants to have a relationship with you. If He already does, continue to draw closer. If He does not, run to Him! Hear His voice, His knock at the door of your heart, and run without looking back. Don't walk. RUN!

Even so, God loves you

John 3:16–17, Hebrews 10:24–25

May 15, 2016 I sit here with tears streaming down my face reading cards people have sent, full of encouraging words, God's promises from His Word, and much love and support – cards, emails, messages, from people I didn't even know have been touched. God is so good! As He pours into my very soul and encourages me through so many, He is also reaching out to those same people and blessing them. We knew God had a bigger plan and purpose – probably beyond what we can even know or imagine. And He is continuing to be in control and bring His plan to fruition.

May Your will be fulfilled in all of this Lord – *whatever You want.* Don't let me stand in Your way. You are my rock and my solid foundation. In Your loving arms I will not be afraid. The following chorus is going through my head today:

"When You don't move the mountains
I'm needing You to move
When You don't part the waters
I wish I could walk through
When You don't give the answers
As I cry out to You
I will trust in You."
(Trust in You by Lauren Daigle)

And also:
"It is well, it is well with my soul."
(It Is Well with My Soul by Horatio Spafford, Philip Bliss)

God is good all the time! All the time God is good – because He uses all things for the good of those who love Him. He does care, and He is here in the midst of everything, using it all to train us, grow us, show His faithfulness, and shine His light through us.

Rough Draft of my song <u>No More Control</u>

Seems so long since I felt Your
Warm embrace,
I need Your Word,
Need Your words to touch my heart.
I so easily turn 'cause I want control.

But no more control Lord,
I give it all to You.
I love Your way,
And I want Your will.
Please lead me Lord Jesus,
Please have Your way in me.

I stand in Your way when I
Take control.
I must let go,
Let go and give You my all.
You are faithful, You don't make mistakes.

So no more control Lord,
I give it all to You.
I love Your way,
And I want Your will.
Please lead me Lord Jesus,
Please have Your way in me.

You have proven Yourself faithful
Time and again,
The solid rock on which I stand.
How can you get the glory when

I won't let go?
Guide me with Your wisdom,
I give you control.

May 15, 2016 (website post) "Finally, brothers and sisters [my dearest brothers and sisters in Christ], whatever is true, whatever is noble, whatever is right, whatever is pure, whatever is lovely, whatever is admirable – if anything is excellent or praiseworthy – think about such things." Philippians 4:8

This is good news! In the midst of all the negative news on TV, the swirling political stories surrounding the upcoming election, the events and circumstances in our lives that are bigger than us – but not bigger than God, there *are* things that are noble, true, just, pure, lovely, and of good report. And in His love for us and knowing what an imperfect world this would be until He returns, He reminds us where our focus should be. He is still here. There is still beauty all around.

I pray we choose to focus on the beauty – not being ignorant of the trouble around us, but keeping it in perspective in this imperfect world. Jesus is our Overcomer, He is faithful to those who have chosen His way and love Him, and this is something awesome for us to meditate on every day – with continual gratitude! God bless you today!

May 17, 2016 I've thought several times about writing today, but struggle with how to relay the mix of emotions that fill my heart – my very soul. It has been a harder time in the hospital for this round, not so much physically as emotionally and spiritually. Not sure of my purpose in this cycle, I find myself restless at a time when I sense God saying, *I just want you to rest, My child.* (Matthew 11:28-30)

Rest. I'm so constantly seeking to pour into others, believing God will pour into me so I can keep pouring out, that I forget to actually apply "Be still and know I am God." (Psalm 46:10) And so God must still me.

I also miss my family immensely. God is gracious and faithful and is providing for all their needs. And my thanks to Him words cannot express. My family is in His hands. They are His and they trust Him. But I miss their company so! I've only gotten to see the kids once this time – Sunday. And Shawn twice – when he stayed Friday night, and then a couple hours Sunday. By the time I get home tomorrow it will have been three long days without them. And though it is true that I need the rest, and the quiet has been good, I long for them. They sound good when I talk to them. I hope it is true when I actually see them and read their faces.

In all this though, when it comes down to it, I want them to treasure Jesus more than anything. I don't know all of God's plan in this, except that He will use this to bring glory to His name and show others the way to Him. Part of His plan could be to take me home, or there may be complications after these cycles that change everything again for our family. Or these events might be paving a new path I am to take (hopefully one that includes writing books that encourage and challenge us).

What I do know – He is in control, and I trust Him fully. And that's good enough for me.

May 18, 2016 Thinking again about the question several friends have asked me, and another friend recently asked again: Do I really have to do the chemo? Isn't there another way? I understand the fears of the chemicals and the side effects, as there is so much research out there about cancer treatments and more natural and safe ways to treat and heal from cancer, and I totally respect that because I believe the research to be true.

I also believe there are times for both kinds of treatment to be used together, and I wonder if part of my journey is to join a path headed to getting oncologists and naturalists and homeopaths working together. Or maybe this path is simply because God needs me here for someone. No matter His plan, in all this the peace that this is the right path for me has not wavered. God has not led me into harm; this is to prosper me in whatever way He wants. I want Him to get the glory for all that happens, for His ways are perfect, His ways are sure. And there is no better place to be than in the center of His will.

A friend sent me this verse this morning: 2 Samuel 22:31 "As for God, His way is perfect. The Lord's word is flawless; He shields all who take refuge in Him."

May 28, 2016 (website post) "We who are strong ought to bear with the failings of the weak and not to please ourselves. Each of us should please our neighbors for their good, to build them up." Romans 15:1-2

Weak - - yes, this is me! After this second cycle, I have been much more tired and have not liked it! There have been many more days where I just do the bare minimum and then all I can do is rest. I'm not sure if I am more tired of the recliner, or the recliner is more tired of me! Some days it is even too much to pick up my phone and text with friends, or call anyone because I feel that weak. Getting a stomach virus on top of it didn't help either. But God is good, and it was only a twenty-four hour virus - which left me, you guessed it, weak!

And yet it is okay to be weak. This is not what we hear in our society. Instead we hear that we must be tough, keep going, pull from the power within us, be in control, etc. And so when we have a weakness, feel powerless in a situation, or face circumstances beyond our control, we feel guilty or like something is wrong with us. But how wonderful does it feel when we can rally around a friend and help them through a tough time? So why can't we be the one who needs to be rallied around sometimes? It is also in these times of needing to just step down, or step back, or just totally rest that we gain a new appreciation for the things around us because we are truly being still. I am enjoying more laughter with my family, and I so enjoy watching them interacting together. I cherish God's Word more, treasure our friends, and hearing the joyful birds each morning brings a bigger smile! And the cards and messages of encouragement that come every day have been a balm to my spirit. My heart is full!

Thank you for being the strong ones that bear with us through this journey, that build me up and encourage me above and beyond! God has used each of you to be here for me, and for us, exactly when we need it, and our appreciation is beyond words.

God bless you and encourage you right where you are! Thank you for walking this journey with us!

> "Frustration is better than laughter, because a sad face is good for the heart." Ecclesiastes 7:3

> "A cheerful heart is good medicine." Proverbs 17:22a

June 1, 2016 Sitting here in the middle of the night wide awake, as sometimes happens right now with the chemo treatment cycles, I am glad I'm not alone. I enjoy writing Thank You's, playing solitaire, praying for family and friends, and just reminiscing, all while talking with You Lord. Thank you for being a constant companion, my First Love, and my best friend. We can talk about anything and everything, and You don't criticize me. You guide me, You love me, You discipline me and pull my focus back when it's off. You laugh with me, You wrap Your arms around me, You give me refuge and a hiding place when I just need to be held or be with You or need a safe place to go in my mind and heart.

I love You Lord. You are my Rock! Thank You Lord!

June 2, 2016 (website post) I sit here with mixed emotions, as I prepare to go in for the third treatment cycle. The peace is still here that God's got this; it's the sadness that I will be away from my family for several days, though they are awesome and have been handling everything GREAT! They are just such a joy to me. It's also the impatience that I just want this to be all done now, plus knowing the tiredness will set in again as my body works to continue healing. And some things I will miss – like going to Kennywood (not that I could handle it right now!) and my oldest playing keyboard with the praise team this Sunday.

Yet in these mixed emotions I have comfort – Jesus went through all the feelings we deal with as humans when He was on earth over two thousand years ago. He knows what I am feeling, and He cares. He will send the right encouragement and the strength needed for each day; I am not alone. He is the One who gets me through!

Praising God in the midst of the storm and drawing closer to Him – not pulling away from Him – is the answer to dealing with how I feel. "For we do not have a high priest who is unable to empathize with our weaknesses, but we have One who has been tempted in every way, just as we are – yet He did not sin. Let us then approach God's throne of grace with confidence, so that we may receive mercy and find grace to help us in our time of need." Hebrews 4:15–16

What do you need today? Have you entrusted it to God? He is your answer. Have a truly blessed day!

June 3, 2016 (website post) Woo-hoo! Great results from the PET scan today – the cancer looks to be gone in my left shoulder and clavicle bone areas, and almost gone in my low spine area. AND the intensity of the cancer in my right shoulder bone has gone down from 35.8 (OUCH!) to a low 4.7, which is almost no pain after what I was feeling! To GOD be ALL the glory for His amazing grace!

This is great news – after only two chemo cycles! It's taking a bit for it to sink in … like something you hope for so badly, and when you receive it, you almost can't believe it. But we choose to believe it.

Can anything still happen? Sure can; let's be realistic. But we choose to move forward believing that God's got this. No matter what His will is, He is still in control. He heals according to His plan, and it is always perfect, even if we don't immediately understand. And what better place to be than in the midst of God's plan!

We are grateful for this great news and hope you are celebrating with us! It's time for a happy dance!

June 4, 2016 I am thinking about the part of the Lord's Prayer "give us today our daily bread." What is your daily bread for today? Remember, just for today – this is *daily* bread. *Matthew 6:11*

For me today:

- Wisdom to decide on pic line – leave it in one more cycle or get a new one
- Food and water
- Joy for the day – God's deep down joy in the midst of the storm
- A shower – which felt wonderful!
- To talk to my family
- Good day with my mom who chose to keep me company all day
- Wisdom to plan ahead regarding my daughter going to a friend's home for a couple days
- Encouragement to stay positive in the storm
- Medicine for nausea
- Quiet time for just me
- To talk with God all day long, knowing He is always with me and will keep my focus right
- Hope for the results of the next cycles to work as well and quickly as the first two cycles
- Bed to sleep on
- Clothes to wear
- Money needed for bills to be paid today
- Energy to exercise and keep myself stretched
- A nap when I get tired

What do you need today? And have you thanked God for your daily bread? Thank Him in advance, believing already that He is answering your prayer and will take care of your daily needs – even the needs you don't yet know you have. God knows. God cares.

Matthew 6:25–34

Comfort zone. The comfort of everything being just right and staying that way. The comfort of being settled in our job, of everything being paid for, or whatever it is that gives us security. The comfort zone can also keep our eyes off God as we are feeling secure in our life and surroundings. Satan likes to subtly blind us to our need for God. For a believer, our comfort zone should be God and God alone. He is the only unchanging thing in our lives. Jobs change, people change, circumstances change, health changes, needs change, and so on. So making our comfort zone anything other than God really does not make sense – even if we do not want to admit it. It is good to feel secure; we need that security. And it is found in God.

Even so, God is forever

Hebrews 13:5–8, James 1:1–18

June 5, 2016 (website post) So today I want to be honest about things I'm feeling – the things I don't necessarily like to share because I want to be the strong one (and must remember it is JESUS who is the strong one in me), but the things I need to share because someone needs encouraged by what I'm about to share.

I do have fears and anxiety with this storm, and questions about some feelings creeping in. I am not strong today – which is when God can be the strongest in me since I can't stand in His way (2 Corinthians 12:9).

Today I'm noticing the nausea is hitting me faster with this third cycle. So does this mean I will be getting sick through the next cycles? And what if God's plan is for me to be done on earth. Have I accomplished all I am supposed to for Him, for His glory? Have I been a good enough wife to my husband; does he know how much I truly love and appreciate him, and how grateful I would be to grow old with him? Have I taught my children enough to help them with this life and to always look to God first? Have I been a good enough friend that they know they are important? And what about this underlying feeling of just wanting to be done – done with this world, tired of being on earth and just wanting to be in heaven with Jesus. Even though He is here with me always, to be in heaven with Him would be so amazingly wonderful! "Better is one day in Your courts than a thousand elsewhere" Psalm 84:10. I'm not even sure I want to be around people. Yet when I am, it is very good! Is it just that I've poured so much into others, that I'm in need of a refill so I have more to pour out again?

Oh Lord, I give all these feelings, anxieties, fears, questions to You, for You understand them. You: my Maker, my Deliverer, my Savior. You know where these come from. And I know that Your perfect love casts out fear (1 John 4:18) Your perfect love encompasses me with Your strength, Your protection, Your joy, Your peace, and does not condemn me.

And in the midst of all these questions there is still Your joy and peace that fill me deep down – the kind that can only come from You because You are Sovereign, You are truth, You are perfection, and You are love – the true and right love. Uncertainties will fill each day, but God never changes – HE is our certainty. Always turn to Him and His wisdom.

Please keep Satan behind me Lord, unable to take these feelings and anxieties and use them to thwart Your plans. By the power of Jesus' name I *know* that Satan is behind me because of Your promise: You are our overcomer (John 16:33). May Your truth and Your words be ever strong in my heart and mind today, pulling me into *Your* will and *Your* desire for me and my life, helping me trust You completely (Proverbs 3:5–6). You have proven again and again in Your Word and in my own life how perfect are Your plans, even though we can't always understand because we don't see the whole picture like You do.

You are Amazing Lord! You are my Rock my Fortress, and the Answer to everything! You are truly the way, the truth, the life. Jesus, You are the one Sovereign Lord. (John 14:6) You are the *only* way. May people flock to You, believing in You, in the name of Jesus, God's Son.

I believe in You always, even in the storm. I love You, my amazing Lord!

June 7, 2016 (website post) It's a beautiful morning as I sit here looking out over the city waiting for breakfast. Hoping I can eat breakfast with this nausea. But it will be okay – the nausea won't last forever, thank goodness! And I'm thinking about the devotion for today: that God will keep us safe, will fight for us. We need to lay our fears and insecurities at His feet and let Him fill us and guide us.

This doesn't mean we won't have troubles; it means we don't have to go it alone. We can be free from the worry and the hold that fear has over us when we let go and let God.

If you are wondering how I stay positive even on the tough days, in the midst of cancer and chemo and side effects, and all the changes this makes for our family right now, it is this: I keep going back to God's Word, His promises, all that He has already done for me in His faithfulness. When we give our life to Jesus Christ, He is truly our overcomer; He is our hope and strength. "I can do all things through CHRIST who gives me strength." Philippians 4:13. "When I am afraid, I put my trust in You." Psalm 56:3

Going to God, reading His words, talking with Him gives me hope, strength, encouragement, every time. And discipline too, for I am far from perfect!

John 14:6 "Jesus said, I am the way and the truth and the life. No one comes to the Father except through Me." Jesus is the answer and the only true way. Trust in Him today!

June 7, 2016 It's a beautiful morning as the sun wakes up the city after a night of rain and storms – such a beautiful view of the skyline and the sun's reflection on all the buildings.

I am focusing this morning on Deuteronomy 3:22, and God's promise to Joshua who would be leading the Israelites into the Promised Land. "Do not be afraid of them [your enemies]; the Lord your God Himself will fight for you." As I read this, I remember another passage where God fought for His servant David. 2 Samuel 5:24 "As soon as you hear the sound of marching in the tops of the poplar trees, move quickly, because that will mean the Lord has gone out in front of you to strike the Philistine army." And again in Proverbs 29:25 God says, "Fear of man will prove to be a snare, but whoever trusts in the Lord is kept safe."

This doesn't mean we won't have struggles and trials and troubles. It means they will not harm and overtake us. "God is our refuge and strength, an ever-present help in times of trouble" Psalm 46:1. And let's look at one more passage: Hebrews 13:5–6 "Keep your lives free from the *love* of money and be content with what you have, because God has said, 'Never will I leave you and never will I forsake you.' So we say *with confidence*, 'the Lord is my helper, I will not be afraid. What can mere mortals do to me?'"

What are your enemies today? What are your fears? These promises are not just for God's people of old. These promises are in His Word to us as an example and a promise to *us*. Whoever believes in Him and chooses to follow Him, these promises are for you! Grasp them, cherish them, praise Him and believe. Look to *Him*.

June 9, 2016 You are my Sovereign Lord. You lift me up when I don't think I can go on, when I'm so tired that my body just aches.

You are my help and my healer. You are my rock. In You there truly is *no* darkness because You are the true light and the only way. I wish people would want to see that Lord, that it is okay that you are the only way. What would sovereignty mean if there were more than one way?

You are my shield, my comfort, my protector, my fortress and my refuge in whom I trust – *with my whole life.* I trust You with *everything -* You Lord, the lover of my very soul. You, who call us to rest in Your love.

I rest in You.

June 11, 2016 On these days when my body is *so* tired and aches so much, and I feel like I can't go on – like my body is shutting down and can't get anymore tired than it already is – these are the days that God wraps me so tightly, as if to say I've got you; you don't need to worry. Whatever I planned for today, just let Me do it.

These are also the days I wonder if I will make it. I so seriously feel like I can't go on, and I think about if God's plan is to take me to heaven. Tears fill my eyes as I think about upcoming things with my family: graduations, birthdays, watching our children start their own adult lives, and all the daily things in between. And of course my wonderful hubby and growing old with him. I hold onto God and let the tears flow. God is always right here for me, no matter what.

When my body feels like this, the physical feeling is almost indescribable, like nothing I've experienced – like my body has just totally shut down – more than the flu, more than a past surgery recovery. How does anyone keep going when their body feels this done? Yet when the exhaustion and 'shut down' subside, my mind clears and I feel like I can do this again, like I can go on. And God immediately has encouragement and strength for me the next day when I can again receive it. He sends me cards, verses, songs to remind me that this is all by His strength and that He's got this. He knows how I feel.

Jesus must have felt like this when He was being beaten, when He was hanging on the cross. He must have been tempted to give up many times – if He would have let His feelings control Him. He says in Hebrews 4 that He has been tempted in every way just as we are – so when He felt like He couldn't go on, felt His body shutting down as He hung to die, He would have been tempted to call the angels to save Him. But instead, He called out to God His Father. He does know how we feel, and so He also knows *exactly what we need.* He truly knows!

I must remember these are feelings. If I let them be in control, I will stand in the way and ruin each day. It is so important to let ourselves feel because it is part of how God made us, but we must keep them in right priority. Give them to the Lord, letting His Spirit be in control of how the feelings affect us and how we handle them. We must let *God* reign in our lives, instead of our feelings. "The weapons we fight with are not the weapons of the world ... we take captive every thought to make it obedient to Christ." 2 Corinthians 10:4–5

May we remain "Joyful in hope, patient in affliction, and faithful in prayer." Romans 12:12

June 16, 2016 (website post) In the song <u>Exhale</u>, sung by Plumb, we are reminded it's okay to not be okay. God is a safe place, and there is still hope as we breathe in His grace and exhale. *(I encourage you to look up the full song)*

This has been a long week of not being okay. I'm not myself, I have no strength – to the point that my legs don't even want to hold me up. I feel so completely helpless. Even though I've rested a lot and pushed through when I needed to, vegetable is the word that keeps coming to mind. I'm so used to being strong that I feel like a limp vegetable. And this song comes to my mind again and again. It's time to rest, breathe in God's grace, feel His arms around me, and exhale. This song has a whole new meaning to me. I hope someone reading this is finding blessing in the song as well, and more importantly in God's grace and love.

After a blood transfusion this week, because we learned that I have become anemic (common with these treatments), I am feeling still very tired, but not like I can't move or function. So I am learning to be even more grateful for the extra rest, trying to learn to stay patient with the healing, and feeling very, very grateful for God's wisdom and patience with me. God is amazing, and God is good – all the time. Praise Him and be blessed!

June 21, 2016 I shouldn't need reminded of all the ways You have been faithful, from the beginning of time, in order for me to trust You. But some days – too many days, I let the circumstances around me latch on, instead of Your power and salvation. I'm sorry Lord. This must hurt You and quench the Spirit, which makes me sad, and makes my heart hurt because I don't want to do that to You, my amazing Lord and Savior. You don't deserve such treatment – ever! How You love us *unconditionally* just blows my mind. You truly are sovereign and amazing! May praise and worship of You continually be on my lips, God my Savior. I love you!
Psalm 91

June 24, 2016 (website post) Well, it has been a long day. Back in for the fourth cycle and we kept hitting roadblocks with my pic line. Short story: had to pull it and I will get a new line in the morning. Of course, it's not what we anticipated; we figured things would be moving along by now and I would be several hours into treatment.

Yet on the other hand it doesn't surprise me. This is part of everyday life – things often don't go how we picture when we start our day. And how do we deal with it?

All day I just kept saying in my head, "I trust Your timing Lord, no matter how frustrating this can be. Help me trust Your plan." This doesn't mean I'm not disappointed. For sure I am. But God must have a reason why that line is not to be used this time. And since He knows everything and is in control, I must let go. Trusting Him does lessen the frustration.

I was also thinking, *I'm already tired from a long day. How much more tired I would be if I waste energy being upset about this. And I want the nurses to want to help me, so no need to snap or get short with anyone. It's just one of those things that happens, and this is not in their control.*

I hope when you have frustrating moments in your day and things don't go as planned, you take a deep breath, tell God you trust His plan, and let it go to Him. Even find something to laugh about – which we did today many times. Laughter refreshes the soul. May you be refreshed as you read this and find hope in God's plan. He loves you!

June 26, 2016 "Cast your cares on the Lord, and He will sustain you; He will never let the righteous to be shaken." Psalm 55:22

As I read this verse this morning, "the righteous shall not be shaken" stands out to me. No matter what we are going through, He will not permit us to be moved. And let's read the first part again, "Cast your cares on the Lord." He expects us to do our part and give Him our load. He doesn't want us to try and go it alone, He doesn't want us to carry our burdens on our own strength. No – He wants to carry them with us so He can keep us from being moved. We really are not alone when we believe in Jesus as our Savior. He lives in us and fills us with His Spirit.

So the next question would be, are we letting Him live in us? Are we doing our part of casting our burdens, our cares, our 'everything' on Him? He is here for us and with us. Letting go – so simple yet so hard. Something I am always working on. But 'letting go' is where it's at! *Matthew 6:25–34*

June 27, 2016 When you feel like writing, but you don't feel like you have much to say, but you try to write anyway – that's me today.

I guess the biggest thought coming to mind today is, how does one explain their joy in the midst of the storms in a way that makes sense? I'm not some perfect angel that has it all together. On the contrary, it is God who holds me together, truly and most definitely! It's in the encouragement and prayers and support that He brings me, through all of you – my family and friends that keep me going, especially when I have grumpy days (yes, I do get grumpy!), days I don't have anything left to pour into people or even want to be around anyone, and days when I'm tired of the storm.

We have weathered many trying storms over the years – hard storms, hard lessons. And the biggest truth from these: *God is faithful.* He is not out to harm us but grow us. He will not let His children, those who believe in Him, fall; He is worthy of our trust and our praise. And through all these times I am learning that what I meditate and focus on, and what I keep telling myself, makes a *huge* difference in my attitude and how each day is handled.

So what do I keep telling myself? I've learned to talk with and listen to God continually, which comes with practice. I'm not perfect at it, but the more I do it and the more intentional I am, the more automatic it becomes, and it is wonderful! It is a great picture of the relationship God has with us. I repeat throughout my day that God is my refuge, strength, fortress, salvation, and that I trust Him. God brings favorite verses to mind, praise songs to my heart, His loving kindness fills my soul. And through all the trials and tests, it helps me to say, "I trust You Lord. You have control." This makes all the difference.

God loves you and He truly has a wonderful plan for you. I hope and pray you find encouragement and truth and hope as you seek Him. You are worth His time and love. He made you! You matter. And you don't have to be perfect or have it all together. He wants to hold you together in His love, and lead and guide you with His truth. You can trust Him. He has the best plan for you!

Psalm 33:11 & 46:1, Proverbs 16:3 & 19:21

How often do we try to avoid going through tough things? But what if going through the tough stuff is exactly what gets us to the next best thing in our lives? What we perceive to be a negative situation may, in fact, be exactly what we must go through to grow and bring us to the next level, or to meet someone God is bringing into our lives, or to open our eyes to His truth. He does allow trials for the furthering of our faith, the strengthening of our patience, and because through our weakness He is strong and can do His best work in us. So let us be thankful in everything.

Even so, God knows best

James 1:2–7, 1 Peter 1:3–9,
2 Corinthians 12:9–10

Ecclesiastes 3:1-8
A Time for Everything

[1] There is a time for everything, and
a season for every activity under the heavens:
[2] a time to be born and a time to die,
a time to plant and a time to uproot,
[3] a time to kill and a time to heal,
a time to tear down and a time to build,
[4] a time to weep and a time to laugh,
a time to mourn and a time to dance,
[5] a time to scatter stones and a time to gather them,
a time to embrace and a time to refrain from embracing,
[6] a time to search and a time to give up,
a time to keep and a time to throw away,
[7] a time to tear and a time to mend,
a time to be silent and a time to speak,
[8] a time to love and a time to hate,
a time for war and a time for peace.

July 19, 2016 Walking through the halls today as I finish up my fifth cycle, I was thinking about how understandable it is that people get depressed in the hospital, especially after being in for so many days. A couple days is okay, but by the fifth day I am wanting out of here! As I walk, sometimes I hear tidbits of what people are going through as doctors are talking in the patient's room, and it makes me sad for them. It's scary too – it could be me going through even more than I already am. Or it could still happen to me. And I pray for them, and for wisdom for the doctors and the team working with them, and for their families. This is not an easy place to have to stay for long.

I am grateful the teams on this floor strive to keep a positive, caring attitude. They genuinely feel for their patients and strive to encourage us and give us a reason to smile.

Thank You Lord for Your gracious hand in all this, for Your blessings in the midst of the storm. Thank You for Your healing presence and for choosing to use me however You will in all this.

Thank You for taking care of my family and for providing for us while I'm off work. And thank You for being my constant companion. I love You and wouldn't want to go through this without You!

July 21, 2016 It's interesting, the feelings and emotions. While there are a plethora of emotions swimming inside me, everything still feels surreal – the fact that I'm sick and all we've been through with it. Everything happened so fast once we got the cancer diagnosis; we just kept moving forward taking the next right steps. And though I've had my share of thoughts and emotions – fear, anxiety, tears, concerns, frustration, exhaustion, not wanting to keep going with the treatments because they're hard, it still feels surreal. And I wonder what all I am *really* feeling. I don't want to push ahead as if it's no big deal, ignoring anything I need to work through.

It's what we often do, isn't it? It seems to be the big push these days: just plow through, you got this, take the bull by the horns, don't slow down you're almost there. Even grieving over the loss of a loved one feels hurried sometimes – you had 3 days now get back to work … you'll get through it. And we wonder why stress is so rampant in our society, why kids are suffering from stress-induced illnesses more than ever, not to mention what it's doing to us as adults.

I read in Psalm 61:1–4 "Hear my cry, O God; listen to my prayer. From the ends of the earth I call to You, I call as my heart grows faint; lead me to the rock that is higher than I. For You have been my refuge, a strong tower against the foe. I long to dwell in Your tent forever and take refuge in the shelter of Your wings." This doesn't sound like someone hurrying through his distress, pushing through the tough stuff and shoving everything else aside because he just needs to keep plowing ahead. King David is overwhelmed and is stopping to dwell in the shelter of the Almighty, crying out to God, letting himself slow down and just be. I pray we all make the time to do this, and teach our children to do this – meditating on Christ and taking in His Word, really living the way He wants for us.

I'm reminded of the song <u>Love Came Down</u> by Kari Jobe:

> "When my heart is overwhelmed
> And I cannot hear Your voice,
> I hold onto what is true
> Though I cannot see…
> I remind myself of all that You've done,
> And the life I have because of Your Son.
> Love came down and rescued me."

Let us be overwhelmed by the Great Almighty!

How awesome that God knows everything about us: our every move, every thought, every motive, everything! This should help us fear God with reverence – there is nothing we can hide from Him. And it should help us embrace following Him more than ever. I mean, don't we want someone leading us who knows us so well that what He has planned fits us perfectly? He knows the best way to help us grow, the best way to use our talents, the best way to speak to us so we hear Him.

Even so, God is God

Psalm 139

July 28, 2016 (website post) Hope: an expectation, a desire for something to happen, trusting something will happen. Hope is a big deal!

As believers in Jesus, we have an *eternal* hope within us. *Within us.* Jesus is our everlasting hope, and He is faithful. He never leaves us.

Hope: even when we turn our back on Him because we choose to go our own way. Jesus is still here and ready to forgive when we confess our sins. What consolation for our imperfect selves. (I John 1:8–9)

Hope: even when we can't see the light at the end of the tunnel. Jesus is still here holding us up with His righteous right hand. (Isaiah 41:10)

Hope: even when things are going well, because we know Jesus is here guiding us in the right path. (Proverbs 3:5–6)

Which brings me to this question today. Are we grasping this hope with both hands, every day? This hope is within us, right here for us to hold onto each day. Do we live like we have hope? Or do we live in fear?

I have a friend who has been battling cancer for the past four years. I remember after just four treatments thinking, "I can't keep doing this." And then I think of him … four years! He has not lost hope. His wife has not lost hope. His son has not lost hope. They choose to get up each day and live because God has given them another day. Even through all the treatments, surgeries, setbacks, infections, in and out of hospitals, this family continues to praise the Lord! They don't blame God. *They run to Him* - - He is their hope.

So I ask again – are we grasping this hope each day, trusting God's plan, or are we letting our circumstances control us? It is my prayer that you are a believer in Jesus – that you have believed on the name of the Lord Jesus Christ, responding to His call to be your Lord and Savior. It is by grace that we are saved, not by anything we do.

Thank You Lord for the gift of sending Your Son to die for us, so we can receive this gift and be with You in heaven some day. You – our ultimate hope!

August 2, 2016 (website post) In my last journal I spoke of a friend who has been battling cancer for four years. He passed away this morning. Please pray for his wife and son as they take one day at a time, grieving their loss. This is an important time of mourning. Jesus also wept over the loss of a dear friend (John 11). I am so glad for them that they are holding onto Jesus. God is their strength. *(Even though this was several years ago, we can still uphold those who have lost loved ones. There are still days of grief and sadness).*

There is also celebration in the midst of this loss, because though we do not get to see him here on earth anymore, he is alive and well in the presence of Jesus because he believed in Him. And he is no longer suffering!

This is not a time to blame God. We all want someone to blame because we want a perfect world. But God did not promise a perfect world. And He did not promise that we would always understand. He did promise to be here for us in the midst of an imperfect world. For believers in Jesus, He is always with us, holding us up with His righteous right hand, helping us grow through the good and the bad, the easy and the hard. He has not left us. I, along with this family, hope you choose to follow Him. He is real!

Thank you for praying for our dear friends. I did not ask permission to use their names here, but God will know for whom you are praying.

August 3, 2016 So I've had these feelings of anxiety for the last two weeks now. Strong anxiety that I feel in the pit of my stomach all the way to my throat. I'm not really sure why. And of course I like to try and figure things out, so I probably add anxiety to it by trying to understand because I want to fix it.

There is part of me that feels like there is a lot to do and I'm not doing enough. Yet I am to be resting. But on the other hand I've been resting for the last couple months and I find myself getting antsy. Maybe I'm nervous about this being the last treatment – not as if anything is going to happen or go wrong. But more like, *what do I do afterward*. Maybe it's just all the emotion of these past months jumbled up inside, since this still seems surreal, and I can't separate all the emotions yet. And I wonder if I'm missing something.

And then there is this annoyance I feel with people. Why are people annoying me? How do I explain it … I'm okay with talking to people for a couple minutes, and then I'm done. I don't want to be around them. What's up with that?

How do I get rid of the jumble of anxiety and emotions? I don't want it sitting in my stomach. I want it out of my system. I feel like a mess.

I feel like there is still so much I need to do with my kids, stuff to teach them and things that need done before they go to school. And every time the anxiety gets stronger, or the emotions get strong, so do my hot flashes. Ugh! I'm sure some of it is just the chemo that is in my system.

In all this I don't want it to be that I'm worried or have stopped trusting God. I still believe He's got this and that He is healing me. I am so grateful for His grace in all this, and all the love and kindness He has shown me, His faithfulness. I don't want to doubt Him or waste my days with worry. Or disobey Him with what He wants me to do.

Lord, You are still my Rock, my Redeemer, my Savior and my Lord. I love You and I need You. Please help me! Father, please help me to feel and to be real, but don't let my emotions control me. Please help me keep everything in perspective.

August 5, 2016 Last treatment! Hooray! I'm so excited, and so far, everything has gone smooth, praise the Lord! Now I just want it to be done. We're praying I won't need radiation. Right now the doctors are saying, "No radiation." Praying and hoping it stays that way.

Still a jumble of emotions. I think part of what I'm feeling has to do with not being able to do much this summer and feeling like I haven't done enough with and for my family. It just seems like there are more things I wanted to teach and show and do with our kids, and the lack of energy and the need to recuperate changed all that. I don't like it.

On the other hand, I had to let go more than I have in the past, let them learn by experience and by trying things. More importantly I've learned to visualize putting them in Jesus' hands again and again. Especially our oldest, who is now twenty. Just when I think I've let go, God shows me I need to let go more. God has him. God has all of us. And I'm so glad. I will mess it up for everyone if I try to stay in control.

Lord, please help me relax in You and trust Your plan. It's not what I wanted for this summer, but Your plans are perfect. Your ways are higher and greater and perfect. I love You, Lord.

August 6, 2016 Such blessings Lord, in the midst of this storm and a different kind of summer. You have given our kids great times with their friends! Right now they're all at our home practicing with their friends for tomorrow's play at church - - not only good for our kids, but also for their friend who just lost his dad. He is in the play too, and it's great to see them supporting him as he strives to move forward with his life. And the other friends who are part of the play are learning more about God through this, and everyone is strengthening their friendships. What a blessing to Shawn and me as we watch them grow and be excited about sharing Jesus!

Shawn and I have also made better time to spend together. We get so caught up in the kids, what needs done, our jobs, that sadly we don't realize how much time we don't spend together. It's been so enjoyable to make time to do special things with and for each other. Just little things. But they mean so much – like a card to say "You're Amazing," a favorite piece of chocolate, surprising him at work with lunch, going for a ride just because, watching a movie together, reading a book together, playing a game together, and more. I love these moments!

And the blessing of extra time with my mom who has travelled here many times to be with us. What great times together! My mom is amazing! All she has done to help with things at home and to be here for me and my family – words can't do justice to how much I appreciate her!

And how about all the people who have rallied around us with love and prayers and encouragement and support and time and help. Amazing!

Like I've said before, God never promised that life would be easy, or fair, or perfect. He promised His plan for my life and yours is perfect, even if we don't understand. Isaiah 55:8–9 "For My thoughts are not your thoughts, neither are your ways My ways," declares the Lord. "As the heavens are higher than the earth, so are My ways higher than your ways and My thoughts than your thoughts." We can't always understand God's perfect ways and His perfect plan because we are not perfect. He sees the whole picture, the big outcome. We must trust Him. Faith is believing without seeing (Hebrews 11:1–2). It's following God and believing in Jesus. Though we haven't seen Him, He has shown Himself in the world around us, and in the Bible, and in our hearts if we choose to listen to Him. But He will not force us to listen; He will not force us to choose Him. He wants a relationship with us, not a band of robots following Him. He wants you. He loves you. Some day He will bring all who love Him and choose Him to perfection and an amazing 'forever' in heaven! But those who do not choose Him, who choose to do life their own way, will not go to heaven. They will go to hell. You see, God is perfect in everything. Which means He is perfect in love, and perfect in justice, and perfect in compassion, and perfect in sovereignty - - perfect in every way, and they all work together perfectly. Again, we cannot understand such perfection because we are not God. But we can choose to follow and trust in Him. He laid down His life for us so we can go to heaven if we choose Him (John 3:16–17). He helps us grow in all the things we go through. He cries with us, celebrates with us, and He will always be with us, be our strength, be our joy and comfort, and be faithful when we choose Him.

Please choose Him. He loves you! Having cancer, having a hard life, doesn't make me want to run from Him; it makes me want to run *to* Him, for He is my strength and joy in the midst of the storm.

I sit here taking in Your words, and I am overwhelmed. I want to cry, and the tears are there, yet they cannot fall. So deep do Your words touch me.

It's not just that You love me, it's not just how much You love me, but how strongly You have wrapped Your arms around me. How jealous You are for my love: "I am jealous for you with a godly jealousy." 2 Corinthians 11:2. You want my full allegiance.

I look at myself; I see how much I want to be more like You. And I see how far I am from that. Your love for us is all because of You, all because You choose to love us. You loved us first.

Oh, if we could but help people see that You do truly love us – ALL of us! You do not force us to love You back; You *call* us to love You. If we choose to go our own way, that is on us, not You. If we choose to believe that we can get to heaven our own way – which would never get us there – instead of just receiving the gift You offer, the one true way to heaven through Jesus, that is on us, not You. But we want someone to blame. Oh Lord, how often You are blamed for our choices. And yet You love us. You love us with a perfect love. Perfect love requires all the parts to be true: justice, mercy, discipline, compassion, etc. ALL the parts. And only You can do this.

Even so, You are the Almighty

Psalm 91, 1 John 4:19

August 8, 2016 (website post) Wow! Here we are at the end of treatments - - one more day and I'm done! I can't even wrap my mind around being done. It's been a different summer, and a whirlwind these last months of being in the hospital, going home, starting to feel better, then back in the hospital … and a jumble of emotions in the midst of it all. God has been so very gracious during this whole journey! Not that the journey is done, but being through the treatments is wonderful! Thank you again for sharing in this with me and my family, for your prayers and encouragement, for being here for us. You all have been amazing!

Last night Shawn and I were able to watch the fireworks after the Regatta in Pittsburgh; so fitting for the end of my treatments. The little things - - don't forget to stop and enjoy the little things in your life. They mean so much, and they help us to slow down and be still from our busy lives. Don't miss them!

May God be gracious in your lives as you choose to follow Him. He loves you and has a perfect plan for you.

Thank you again, our dear friends, for everything! I will keep you posted as I begin to really recuperate. Praising God in ALL things!

August 8, 2016 Oh Lord, You have given me this opportunity to recoup; to just have extra time with You, to not be needed as much right now after all the over-pouring I have done into other's lives without stopping to be poured back into myself – which exhausted me and didn't teach a good pattern to my family. Why do we push through? You didn't put "Be still and know that I am God" in the Bible for no reason (Psalm 46:10). You knew we would need reminded that You are on the throne, that we don't have to do it all, but rather be still and hear Your call and just do what You ask.

Be still – how easy it is to get annoyed by these words. In our humanness we think we have to keep going, keep striving, that we have to figure it all out, that success is in how much we do, how much we accomplish. When really, success is measured in You and Your accomplishments in our lives that bring glory to You.

Lord, may we look at *be still* in a better light. May we slow down and let You live in and through us the way You planned and in a way that brings the glory back to You. It's not about us and what we do. It's all about You, our amazing, awesome, Sovereign Lord! We love You!

Have you ever read Psalm 131? "My heart is not proud, O Lord, my eyes are not haughty. I do not concern myself with great matters or things too wonderful for me. But I have calmed and quieted my soul, I am like a weaned child with its mother; like a weaned child I am content. O Israel, put your hope in the Lord both now and forevermore."

What a great chapter to meditate on! Not because it's only three verses, but because of the power in these verses. Read it again; take in its very meaning. We would hope to truly say of ourselves that we are not haughty and proud. But how about the next part: "I do not concern myself with great matters, things too wonderful for me." Knowledge and understanding are good, and God wants us to desire them of Him. Yet how often do we stress over the things that we really cannot understand? Understanding God is something we strive for, but we also need to be okay with the fact that we will never totally understand Him ... He is God! How often do we say, "But Lord, I want to understand the why and how of this situation!" And He gently reminds us that He is in control. Let us still and quiet our souls and totally let go, allowing Him to fill us with the understanding that He gives, totally and completely trusting Him with everything – because He is God.

Even so, He quiets my soul

Proverbs 2:1–6

August 12, 2016 It's not about how easy we can make our life; it's about growing through the hard stuff and following God in this imperfect world. As a believer in Jesus, it's not about how successful *we* are, but did we stay open to God's plan and Him working through us, which brings Him glory. He is God. All-powerful, magnificent, glorious and sovereign, a just and loving God who always has been and always will be. He deserves our praise just because He is, just because He made us, just because He loves us. He loves us no matter what! We don't have to clean up our act and then come to Him. We come to Him in total repentance and admit our need of Him, which starts a relationship with Him, and He helps us clean up our life.

God says in His all-inspired Word (2 Timothy 3:16–17) that no one is good, not one. (Psalm 14:1–3; Psalm 53:1–3; Romans 3:12) We may look good, look like we have it all together, be the nicest person on the face of the earth. But until our desires and motives are in line with pleasing Him, we are still selfish and focused on ourselves. It is He who makes us good through the blood of His Son Jesus – the perfect Lamb, the perfect sacrifice for all. We just need to accept His sacrifice.

He stands knocking at the door of our hearts, wanting a beautiful relationship with each of us. But though it's what He wants, He will not force it. He doesn't want us to go through this life without Him. But we must choose Him. He chooses us and we choose Him – that's when the relationship is real.

Can you imagine sacrificing your only son so people can have eternal life in heaven with you, in the perfect world you want to give them, and instead people protest, put up their hand, say, "No thanks, that sacrifice doesn't mean anything"? But we are not perfect people. When Adam and Eve chose to go their own way in the Garden, instead of follow God, sin entered the world (Genesis 3). Yet God had a plan to offer redemption to anyone who will receive. He is calling out to you. Will you receive Him? (John 1:9–13; Romans 3:22–24; Romans 6:22–23)

2 Timothy 3:16–17 "All Scripture is God-breathed and is useful for teaching, rebuking, correcting and training in righteousness, so that the servant of God may be thoroughly equipped for every good work."

The Bad News:

Psalm 14:1–3 and Psalm 53:1–3 "The fool says in his heart, 'There is no God.' They are corrupt, their deeds are vile; there is no one who does good. The Lord looks down from heaven on all mankind to see if there are any who understand, any who seek God. All have turned away, all have become corrupt; there is no one who does good, not even one."

Romans 3:12 "All have turned away, they have together become worthless; there is no one who does good, not even one."

The Good News:

Revelation 3:20 "Here I am! I stand at the door and knock. If anyone hears My voice and opens the door, I will come in and eat with that person, and they with Me."

John 1:9–13 "The true light that gives light to everyone was coming into the world. He was in the world, and though the world was made through Him, the world did not recognize Him. He came to that which was His own, but His own did not receive Him. *Yet to all who did receive Him, to those who believed in His name,* He gave the right to become children of God – children born not of natural descent, nor of human decision or a husband's will, but born of God."

Romans 3:22–24 "This righteousness is given through faith in Jesus Christ to all who believe. There is no difference between Jew and Gentile, for all have sinned and fall short of the glory of God, and all are justified freely by His grace through the redemption that came by Christ Jesus."

Romans 6:22–23 "But now that you have been set free from sin [when you believe on the name of the Lord Jesus Christ] and have become slaves of God, *the benefit you reap leads to holiness, and the result is eternal life.* For the wages of sin is death, but the gift of God is eternal life in Christ Jesus our Lord."

Romans 10:9–13 "If you declare with your mouth that 'Jesus is Lord,' and believe in your heart that God raised Him from the dead, you will be saved. For it is with your heart that you believe and are justified, and it is with your mouth that you profess your faith and are saved. As Scripture says, 'Anyone who believes in Him will never be put to shame.' For there is no difference between Jew and Gentile – the same Lord is Lord of all, and richly blesses all who call on Him, for 'Everyone who calls on the name of the Lord will be saved.'"

August 18, 2016 (website post) That moment when you think you are just going to mingle and say hello to people and thank them for all their encouragement and support, and then you're being handed a microphone to stand in front of all of them and talk! But what a great opportunity to thank a beautiful group of people who surrounded us in amazing ways – my Trinity family!

We want to thank EVERYONE who has been part of our journey in any way. The prayers, encouragement, support and help have truly gone beyond what we imagined; my own amazing family, parents, brothers and sisters, our church family at Living Stone Community, my family at Trinity, families where Shawn teaches piano, friends and friends of friends … we don't want to miss anyone in our message of thanks – this is to ALL of you!

Finding ways to be thankful has so helped keep tough times from totally overwhelming me; God does tell us to be thankful in everything. Having all of you stand with us has been a HUGE part of our thankfulness.

I'm still at a loss for the words to express our gratefulness. We hope you know it sincerely comes from deep in our hearts. THANK YOU for walking this journey with us!

August 25, 2016 (website post) My body seems to be gearing up to go in the hospital for another treatment, like it has for the past couple months. Tomorrow would be the next round if I had to go in. But praise God I am done with the treatments! Now if my body would just realize it. This week has been bouts of anxiety and just feeling 'off', and God has given me these verses to continually guide me through:

Psalm 94:18–19 "When I said, 'My foot is slipping,' your unfailing love, Lord, supported me. When anxiety was great within me, Your consolation brought me joy."

I Peter 5:6–7 "Humble yourselves, therefore, under God's mighty hand, that He may lift you up in due time. Cast all your anxiety on Him because He cares for you."

Philippians 4:6–7 "Do not be anxious about anything, but in every situation, by prayer and petition with thanksgiving, present your requests to God. And the peace of God, which transcends all understanding, will guard your hearts and your minds in Christ Jesus."

I am learning to take whatever is on my mind and picture it as a big ball I am placing in God's hands. The cool thing is, as I visualize placing it in His hands, the ball of stuff becomes small because God is so big, the burdens lift, and I feel free to move forward with what I'm supposed to focus on, leaving everything up to Him. It's amazing how God does this when we choose to give it to Him.

I have to give Him the ball of stuff again and again, because I'm really good at giving it up and then grabbing it back, trying to be in control or make my timing happen. But I feel so much better when I let it go and trust Him. And I hope you find this to be true for you too.

May God meet you where you are today, and every day. And may each of us be willing to let go, trust Him, and ask Him to fill us with His wisdom. He's just waiting for us to ask – James 1:5

September 10, 2016 (website post) I've been wanting to write again and share with you as I'm recuperating, but each time it's been a jumble of thoughts that I can't separate. Having to chill out and rest extra, sometimes gives one too much thinking time. I have found it helps to listen to uplifting Christian music and spend time reading the Bible, so I'm not getting overwhelmed or depressed as my mind races. But there is one thing I have been thinking about a lot after this battle with lymphoma: are there things I need to change in my lifestyle. Of course the answer is yes because we are always improving ourselves.

As I've prayed about this and talked with some friends, it's become evident that I need to make better time for myself. I love pouring into others, and yes, we are to be about serving others. But God doesn't mean for us to ignore our own needs in the process. However, I tend to do that. So I'm learning to make better time for exercising, and to give myself quiet time before going to bed (instead of feeling guilty for putting my feet up when there are still things to do). Continually pouring out without stopping can bring one dangerously close to going the other extreme of not wanting to be there for anyone at all. Having cancer made me *have* to slow down and realize how exhausting a path I was traveling, and I need God to help me create a different harmony in what I choose to do each day.

I am thankful for the lessons and the blessings in each storm in my life, and I hope you can say the same in your life. Storms require us to listen more to God as He guides us through each day; they keep us seeking Him because we will find Him when we seek Him with all our heart (Jeremiah 29:13). And we will trust Him more and grow even closer to Him, which is such a great blessing. May you see God's goodness in the storms in your life, and may the greatest blessing be in growing closer to Him.

September 14, 2016 I haven't written as much these past weeks it seems. It's been a jumble of things happening, getting back into some sort of structure and trying to rest enough but still do what I need to do. It hasn't been easy.

My body had settled into a new structure that went with the chemo treatments. Then they ended but I still tired easily, so there wasn't really any kind of structure for about a month. Now I am getting a little more energy and have also started physical therapy for my shoulder; so I can add some structure, but I still have a few days where I just stay in bed all day.

It also means a lot of time to think. And the enemy, Satan, likes to sneak those lies in, bringing up the past and bringing in guilt, or making me believe that I'm not enough or won't be enough. He tries to make me believe that the mistakes I've made will forever hurt the people I love. And he tries to get me to question my purpose here. Do I have a purpose anymore? This brings anxiety and depression. And I forget to be thankful. And my focus turns to me instead of God.

This is why God reminds us to be thankful in everything and to cast all our cares on Him. He knows what we need, and He wants to help us through. But if we don't fix our eyes on Him we miss out on His guidance and His tender mercies, which are new every morning. We need to keep picturing ourselves putting everything back in His hands. It's when we let go, and when we return to being thankful in everything, that we find freedom instead of weight on our shoulders. And we find the blessings even in the storms, even in the really bad storms.

I have a friend who lost his wife unexpectedly last week. He and their children have quite a storm they are going through right now, and I can't imagine the pain and suffering in their hearts. Yet he is still able to say that God is going to bring good out of all this. Another reminder that God is good even when we don't understand, and here even in the storms.

Have you ever found yourself on one side of things asking 'where is the blessing', and later on the other side asking 'why the blessing'? Several years ago I found myself on the first side wondering if the storms would ever break and where was the blessing. In God's grace He continued to show there were still blessings in the storm and He taught me to trust Him so much more than I ever had. Now I find myself on the other side asking why the blessing. Why has my life been spared in the cancer, but my friend's was not. And God reminds me that His plan is perfect in all situations, even when we don't see it. He shows the blessings that are real even in the loss of a loved one.

I feel guilty sometimes being around our friends who lost this loved one, wondering if I make things harder on them, as they see me doing so well. But they don't show bitterness. They continue to rejoice with me about my good reports, and we continue to pray and praise together. This is God. This is God being good and being here. He is real and He is still here with us, no matter what comes. We praise You Lord!

"Show me Your ways, Lord, teach me Your paths. Guide me in Your truth and teach me, for You are God my Savior, and my hope is in you all day long. Remember, Lord, Your great mercy and love, for they are from old." Psalm 25:4–6

"As for God, His way is perfect: the Lord's word is flawless; He is a shield to all who take refuge in Him." Psalm 18:30

"Let the peace of Christ rule in your hearts, since as members of one body you were called to peace. And be thankful." Colossians 3:15

Life isn't about us.
It's about life in Christ.
It's about God's grace.
It's about Jesus.

Hebrews 10:23–24

"Let us hold unswervingly to the hope we profess, for He who promised is faithful. And let us consider how we many spur one another on toward love and good deeds."

He who promised … of all the promises God has given, a struggle-free life is not one of them. But a faithful God IS!

Even so, God is good

September 19, 2016 It's interesting sometimes, how guilt plays with our minds. I have really struggled these past weeks with feeling guilty for making it through my cancer while our beloved friend passed away from complications with his, which I alluded to the last time I wrote. But then I also feel jealous because I want to see Jesus now too. I'm tired of this messed up world and just want Jesus to call us all home. And then I feel guilty for wanting to be in heaven because I still have a family here that I don't want to leave behind – which is why I just want Jesus to take all the believers now. What a cycle of thoughts in my head. I need to turn my mind off – time for a mental power outage.

Thankfully God always has a way of fixing our focus. A friend recently reminded me that God's plan for each person is perfect, and that right now I am to be a symbol of hope and a *living* testimony of God's goodness and power. Someone somewhere needs to be encouraged by all God is doing, needs to see God's goodness and be reminded that it is all around us, even in the midst of the wickedness and selfishness that is so prevalent in our world today. We have to want to see the good, and then we will find it. Just like we have to want to see God, then we will find Him.

Jeremiah 29:13 "You will seek Me, and you will find Me when you seek Me with all your heart."

Deuteronomy 4:29 "But if from there you seek the Lord your God, you will find Him if you seek Him with all your heart and with all your soul."

September 23, 2016 (website post) What a plethora of emotions this week as I approached today's PET scan! I could feel the anxiety levels rising as the possibilities ran through my head. Yes, God is in control. Yes, His plan could also be different from what I want. And so letting go and relaxing in His control has been a struggle this week, striving to be okay with God's will.

Yesterday I reached out to many of you for extra prayers, and God's peace covered me so wonderfully as you all prayed and encouraged me. THANK YOU! You each are such a blessing to us – truly! I fell asleep last night thanking God for all of you and thinking of verses and praise songs.

And the results of today's scan … everything is clear! I am considered cancer free! No more chemo treatments, just recuperating and easing back into 'normal' life. Talk about a plethora of emotions: I could sing, dance, cry, shout, laugh, and fall on my knees in gratitude to God, all at the same time! TO GOD BE THE GLORY! I am so very grateful for His healing grace; words can't do justice for the gratitude we all feel.

Thank you for being with us. I don't know if I'm done journaling yet. There still may be more to share. But again, thank you everyone. May this bring you hope and joy, reminding that, even so, God journeys with us through the storms.

September 27, 2016 (website post) Thinking back this morning to a conversation with a friend about a month ago: I had asked if after her cancer, she found herself questioning and second-guessing everything she did, not wanting to do anything that would cause the cancer to return. She said she struggled with the same thing, and it took a while to relax and stop doing that. I already over-analyze most things, so each day is *over*-filled with second guessing everything I do. UGH! This is something I definitely need to stop doing.

This past Sunday our Pastor made a great point: as Christians we can believe, without even seeing it, that God has prepared a place in heaven for those who believe in His Son, Jesus Christ – without even seeing it! Yet we have trouble trusting that He will take care of us and guide us in the here and now, no matter what our struggles: finances, relationships, anxieties, health problems, our thorns in the flesh, and so on.

Here is a Sovereign God reaching down to us so we can follow Him – He's got this – and we fuss and worry and fret over situations that are never too much for Him. From the littlest things to the very biggest things. He already knows how to work it all out for our good. It's easy to keep looking at it all through our own eyes; Satan loves to distract and discourage us like this. *(Read John 10:1-18)*

Our struggles are like a helium-filled balloon; we hold onto it, weight it down so it can't go anywhere. We look at it, poke it, bat it around, but it stays in its place under our control. What would happen if we let it go? It might fall to the ground. It might go really high. It might go so far and then pop. But it went somewhere. If we let our struggles go into God's hands, some things may fall to the ground, some things may go really far, and some things might pop in our face – BUT – it will be according to God's plan and we will be free! Free from these burdens we keep holding down, and free to serve God with all our hearts.

Jesus said in John 8:32 "You will know the truth and the truth will set you free." He does not want us to be slaves to our sin – like worrying and fretting. He does not want us to be slaves to our burdens. Matthew 11:28–30 "Come to Me, all you who are weary and burdened, and I will give you rest. Take My yoke upon you and learn from Me, for I am gentle and humble in heart, and you will find rest for your souls. For My yoke is easy and My burden is light."

"Cast all your cares on Him, for He cares for you." 1 Peter 5:7 Why not take the time right now to list your cares, and then, with thanksgiving, give them to God:

_____   _____

_____   _____

_____   _____

_____   _____

_____   _____

September 28, 2016 Oh, how hard it is to watch a loved one go through hard times, and all we can do is pray for them and be there with them. Not even words can help; actually, words just make it worse at this moment. We wish we could take their suffering away, but God did not promise that life would be easy. He did promise to be faithful and to work all things for the good of those who love Him (Romans 8:28). Yet, how often that doesn't seem like enough, just knowing the promises. We want to fix it, to do more, to walk them through and out of their storm immediately – like the short ten minute storms we sometimes get here in the summer. But we would be taking our eyes off God and not trusting Him if we grabbed control like that. And we would mess it all up.

I'm reminded of when a caterpillar becomes a butterfly – the caterpillar struggles and works hard to break out of his cocoon; it is quite a process for him. But if we would, in feeling sorry for him, make it easier by breaking the cocoon open and fixing what seems like a problem, he would not be able to fly. For it is in the hard work, the struggle to break out, that his wings gain their strength. And so it is with us: the hard work, the struggles give our wings their strength so we can fly.

God knows what we need, and He knows how each storm, each moment in our lives will make us stronger in Him, more trusting of Him, and more convinced that nothing can separate us from His love – not even the strongest storm (Romans 8:38–39).

God is good, even in the storms.

October 23, 2016 I'm starting my fourth week back to work now, praise the Lord! I'm tired, but a good tired if that makes sense. After five months of having to slow down, fight off cancer, rest and recuperate, getting back in a routine is good but also has its challenges. Like taking the changes I've had to make, and keeping them applied now that days are much fuller. We blink and our schedules fill up with work, physical therapy, basketball, household chores, etc. We all feel it. But do we make for ourselves a time each day to slow down? Hopefully we are having quiet time with God each day, which is the best quiet time ever! And time to just be.

This kind of quiet time became a norm in my life when I was in the hospital for five days at a time and then home resting, and I learned to enjoy it. I realize how much I need it compared to how much I was actually allowing myself to have it. It's so easy to get caught up in the 'I have to' of the day and our only quiet time is when we fall into bed at night. Talk about stress and exhaustion; that will surely add to it!

Thinking about tomorrow being Monday, I have to say I am not dreading work; I have great people to work with! I know not everyone likes their job, or likes getting up in the morning, or maybe you have tough situations waiting at the office or at home. I get that. And I think about people I know and the ways they approach their days. What is our frame of mind each morning when we awake? Are we immediately caught up in the 'I HAVE to' or do we approach the days with 'I GET to'? Do we walk outside and breathe in the fresh air? Do we turn on music and praise the Lord as we start our day? Or are we complaining and focusing on everything that isn't right?

Quiet time with God, quiet time for the soul, quiet time for our mental state. And in all of it, giving each day to the Lord.

Let us challenge ourselves and each other to follow through.

November 10, 2016 A couple months ago, while I was still going through chemo treatments for my lymphoma, my daughter painted a simple canvas for me with this message: Live.

It's amazing how one word can touch a soul so very deeply; it still brings tears to my eyes. And it reminds me every day to choose to live. Not just to physically live through the day, but also choose to *really* live!

As each day brings its own challenges, what do we choose? Do we choose to be happy, to enjoy each day? Yes, there is trouble in the world, there are struggles each day. Jesus said there would be in John 16:33. And He also said "Take heart. I have overcome the world." God doesn't want us to live our days in fear, to worry, fret and complain. Philippians 2:14 "Do everything without grumbling and arguing." Psalm 118:24 "...let us rejoice *today* and be glad." Choose joy, choose life, choose hope!

I am thinking of the simple blessings around me: my husband, my children, family and friends, nature, laughter, comfort, food, our senses, music, coffee, chocolate, and the list goes on. We have so many reasons to enjoy life! Life is hard, but it's not the end. Even if we have to look harder, we can find reasons to rejoice. If this weren't true God would not have told us in 1 Thessalonians 5:16–18 "Rejoice always, pray continually, give thanks in all circumstances; for this is God's will for you in Christ Jesus."

So what will you choose?

December 25, 2016 Every day is a journey. How is yours going? Especially during the Christmas holiday, it's so easy to get caught up in the extra events – Christmas plays, Christmas concerts, extra trips to stores for just the right gift, planning get-togethers, baking, and more. I find myself many times having to sit down and remind myself to enjoy each event, enjoy all the steps in each day's journey, instead of making it a list of to-do's that I just need to cross off.

Several times over the past week coming up to Christmas day, I've thought about the journey Joseph and Mary had to Bethlehem, and the journey from when Mary was first told she had been chosen by God to bear His Son Jesus. I wonder if she had an easy pregnancy. I also wonder if that journey to Bethlehem was difficult – pregnant and riding cross country. But I don't expect she complained. And this is what stands out to me.

This week we continue our journey that started just over a year ago with the tumor in my shoulder: the every three months PET scan to confirm my cancer is not returning. For a couple days last week I found worry sneaking its way into my mind; I surely don't want to go through that again. But as I turn my attention to Jesus, His peace continues to fill me, just as the angels voiced to the shepherds when Jesus was born – good news for all people ... peace on earth. The peace that Jesus puts in our hearts when we believe in Him is the peace we can have on earth in the midst of our daily journeys. And how freeing! This peace frees me from the worries that try to take hold.

We wish this same peace for you; we pray you know the peace of Jesus, deep in your very soul, through each step of your journey.

"But we have this treasure in jars of clay to show that this all-surpassing power is from God and not from us. We are hard pressed on every side, but not crushed; perplexed, but not in despair; persecuted, but not abandoned; struck down, but not destroyed. Therefore we do not lost heart. Though outwardly we are wasting away, inwardly we are being renewed day by day. For our light and momentary troubles are achieving for us an eternal glory that far outweighs them all. So we fix our eyes not on what is seen, but on what is unseen, since what is seen is temporary, but what is unseen is eternal." 2 Corinthians 4:7–9, 16–18

Even so, He is with us through the journey

About the Author

Trisha Caldwell has enjoyed writing for smaller publications and newsletters over the past twenty years, and is ready to share her storm with you, in the hopes that you will find strength and courage in your storms. Trisha lives with her family in Pennsylvania and continues to enjoy life and writing.

Other Books:

- Add to Your Faith
- Playing With the Moon
- The Whispering Moon (watch for release date!)

* Find inspiration & updates at TuesdaysLunchCup.com *

Printed in the United States
by Baker & Taylor Publisher Services